Fern Green

photography by Deirdre Rooney

POWER

MILKS

hardie grant books

CONTENTS

INTRODUCTION

Most of us are big fans of coffee but how about an energising alternative? Perhaps you are fed up with the caffeine jitters and want something that boosts you with plant power instead?

The power milk has been born and is here to stay. Packed with superfoods, herbs, roots and spices from ancient and traditional cultures, these are mixed with non-dairy milks. Sound appealing?

Perhaps you suffer from an afternoon slump and are fed up with drinking more coffee. Maybe you are looking for something with a healthy nutritious boost, either hot or cold, to satisfy your taste buds?

There are over 60 recipes of delicious hot and cold power plant-based milk drinks in this book to explore. They have been especially created to help awaken your senses, elevate your mind and enhance your day-to-day health. These drinks also help increase your immune function, have anti-ageing effects, improve stamina and athletic performance as well as help to improve your liver function and detoxification.

PLANT-BASED MILKS

This book includes a variety of non-dairy milks. It is possible to buy them, but it's better to make your own. Here are some recipes to start you off. The maple syrup is optional and the milks can be chilled for 2–3 days.

Hazelnut

Makes: 4 – Prep: 5 minutes + Soak: overnight

YOU NEED
500 g raw hazelnuts • 2 tablespoons maple syrup

Soak hazelnuts in 2.5 cm water for 12 hours, or overnight. Drain and rinse, then blitz in a blender with 500 ml water until smooth. Strain milk through a nut milk bag or muslin. Add syrup.

Cashew

Makes: 4 – Prep: 5 minutes + Soak: overnight

YOU NEED
600 g raw cashews • pinch of sea salt • 2 tablespoons maple syrup

Soak cashews in 2.5 cm water for 12 hours, or overnight. Drain and rinse, then blitz in a blender with 600 ml water until smooth. Strain milk through a nut milk bag or muslin. Add salt and syrup.

Almond

Makes: 4 – Prep: 5 minutes + Soak: overnight

YOU NEED
500 g raw almonds • pinch of sea salt • 2 tablespoons maple syrup

Soak almonds in 2.5 cm water for 12 hours, or overnight. Drain and rinse, then blitz in a blender with 500 ml water until smooth. Strain milk through a nut milk bag or muslin. Add salt and syrup.

Oat

Makes: 2 – Prep: 5 minutes + Soak: 3 hours

YOU NEED
600 g rolled oats • 2 teaspoons vanilla extract

Soak oats in water for 3 hours. Drain and blend with 600 ml water until smooth. Stir in vanilla extract and strain milk through a nut milk bag or muslin.

Brazil

Makes: 3–4 – Prep: 5 minutes + Soak: 2 hours

YOU NEED
130 g Brazil nuts • 4 Medjool dates, pitted • pinch of sea salt • 1 teaspoon vanilla extract

Soak Brazil nuts in water for 2 hours. Drain and blend with remaining ingredients and 1 litre water until smooth. Strain through a nut milk bag or muslin.

SPECIAL INGREDIENTS

Here are some of the super fruit, herb and mushroom powders that are used in this book to enhance the plant-based milks. They are a convenient way of adding antioxidants into your power milks. You can buy them all online.

Maqui berry – This dark purple berry is grown in southern Chile. It is low calorie, low carbohydrate and full of antioxidants.

Camu Camu – These berries are nature's richest source of vitamin C in addition to other antioxidants, such as anthocyanins, flavonols and ellagic acid.

Lucuma – This Peruvian stone fruit contains iron, zinc, calcium and protein. Its maple-like taste makes it a sweet addition.

Sea Buckthorn – These berries are packed with protein-building amino acids, lots of vitamins, minerals, healthy fatty acids and carotenoids; all of which are super good for you!

Baobab Powder – Packed full of vitamins C and B6, calcium, potassium and thiamin. The vitamin C contributes towards reduction of tiredness and a healthy immune system and skin.

Ashwagandha – This is one of the powerful herbs used in Ayurvedic healing and is well-known for its restorative benefits. It is commonly used to help with stress, fatigue and lack of energy.

Fo-ti – This herb is used in Chinese medicine as a tonic for longevity. It can help digestion and skin problems.

Reishi – This mushroom powder has several benefits, from improving liver function, detoxification and promoting heart health to balancing blood pressure.

Cordycep – These mushrooms are said to be a natural aphrodisiac. They also help increase immune function, have anti-ageing effects, improve stamina and detoxification.

Chaga – This is not a mushroom but a fungus, which grows on the birch trees of Siberia, Alaska and Northern Canada. High in antioxidants, it helps with energy levels.

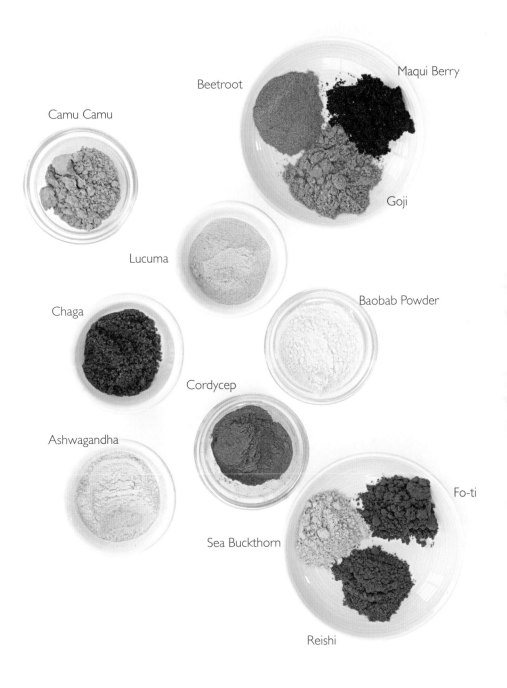

Camu Camu

Beetroot

Maqui Berry

Goji

Lucuma

Baobab Powder

Chaga

Cordycep

Ashwagandha

Fo-ti

Sea Buckthorn

Reishi

HOW TO CREATE YOUR OWN FROTHY MILK

All of the hot milk recipes can be frothed to create a creamier, thicker finish if desired. If you have always fancied yourself as a barista, and would like to create special milk art on your drinks, try the tips below.

Making milk art at home

When creating milk art there are three things to remember:

- Always use a jug to pour the milk into your desired cup or mug.
  A stainless steel one seems to be popular for baristas.
- Frothed milk should be between 60–71°C.
- Practise, practise, practise.

Three suggested frothing tools

Frothing wand – This budget option is simple to use for whipping up small amounts of hot milk. Warm the milk, then lower the wand into the milk and whisk for 3–5 minutes until the milk is as frothy as you would like. This can be found online or in kitchen stores.

Non-electric milk frother or French press – This is a medium range frother, which uses a jug on the hob. You need to pump the plunger a few times to make frothy milk.

Electric milk frother – This machine can prepare hot and cold frothy milk easily. It is worth buying one that is slightly more expensive as the cheaper versions won't last that long.

The heart stencil

Step 1

Froth your milk and cut out a heart
shape from a clean bit of cardboard.

Step 2

Pour the frothed milk on top
of your drink.

Step 3

Hold the heart template above the drink
and sprinkle your powder over the top
(beetroot powder was used here).

Step 4

Decorate with dried rose petals or
extra powders for a colourful finish.

JUICE MILKS

These juices are made by mixing plant-based milks with specially formulated juices to give your body a boost and awaken your senses. Please note that you will need a juicer to create the recipes marked with a *.

Spiced Apple • Sweet Potato
Turmeric Coco • Turmeric Kick • Honey Lemon
Pomegranate • Goji Berry • Mocha Maca
Green Banana • Coffee Almond • Warm Mango
Beetroot Cacao • Earthy Almond
Blueberry Flax • Berry Baobab
Simple Green • Super Kale

SPICED APPLE*

Makes: 1
Preparation: 5 minutes

YOU NEED

1 carrot, chopped • 1 apple, cored and quartered
1 cm piece of fresh ginger, peeled • 1 tablespoon apple cider vinegar
1 teaspoon honey • pinch of ground cinnamon
pinch of cayenne pepper • coconut milk, to top up

Apple cider vinegar can help kill many types of bacteria as well as lowering blood sugar levels.

D *Aids digestion*   **I** *Immunity boosting*   **V** *Vitamin rich*

Juice the carrot, apple and ginger and pour into a jug. Add the vinegar, honey, cinnamon and cayenne and stir. Top up to 300 ml with coconut milk.

SWEET POTATO*

Makes: 1
Preparation: 5 minutes

YOU NEED
1 sweet potato, chopped • 1 apple, cored and quartered
¼ teaspoon ground cinnamon • 1 teaspoon maple syrup • almond milk, to top up

Sweet potatoes are packed full of vitamins including vitamin C. They are also a good source of potassium, which is a great boost for a healthy heart.

(V) *Vitamin rich* (C) *Calming* (E) *Energising*

Juice the sweet potato and apple and pour into a jug. Add the cinnamon and maple syrup and stir. Top up to 300 ml with almond milk.

TURMERIC COCO*

Makes: 1
Preparation: 5 minutes

YOU NEED
½ teaspoon ground turmeric • ½ lemon, peeled • 1 cm piece of fresh ginger, peeled
1 teaspoon honey • coconut milk, to top up

Turmeric contains curcumin, which is a good anti-inflammatory.
It is perfect if you are suffering from a cold, flu or fatigue.

A *Alkalising* **B** *Blood stimulating* **I** *Immunity boosting*

Juice the turmeric, lemon and ginger and pour into a jug. Add the honey.
Top up to 300 ml with coconut milk.

TURMERIC KICK*

Makes: 1
Preparation: 5 minutes

YOU NEED

½ teaspoon ground turmeric • 1 orange, peeled • 1 cm piece of fresh ginger, peeled
1 teaspoon honey • pinch of cayenne pepper • rice milk, to top up

Cayenne pepper helps aid digestion and boosts the metabolism.

A *Anti-inflammatory* **V** *Vitamin rich* **B** *Blood stimulating*

Juice the turmeric, orange and ginger and pour into a jug.
Add the honey and cayenne. Top up to 300 ml with rice milk.

HONEY LEMON

Makes: 1
Preparation: 5 minutes

YOU NEED
1 teaspoon honey • juice of ½ lemon
pinch of cayenne pepper • splash of almond milk

Lemons contain potassium, which is beneficial for a healthy heart.

A *Alkalising*   **M** *Metabolism boosting*   **V** *Vitamin rich*

Put the honey, lemon and cayenne into a glass and add 250 ml water.
Add the almond milk and serve.

POMEGRANATE

Makes: 1
Preparation: 5 minutes

YOU NEED

300 ml almond milk • 1 tablespoon unsalted cashews
1 tablespoon almond butter • 1 teaspoon pomegranate powder

Pomegranates are a great source of vitamins A, C, E and folic acid.

V *Vitamin rich* **P** *Protein boosting* **M** *Mineral rich*

Put all the ingredients into a blender and blend until smooth.

GOJI BERRY

Makes: 1
Preparation: 5 minutes

YOU NEED
300 ml cashew milk • 1 tablespoon unsalted cashews
1 tablespoon dried goji berries • 1 tablespoon cashew butter
pinch of ground cinnamon

Goji berries promote healthy skin and help stabilise blood sugar levels.

P *Protein boosting* **M** *Metabolism boosting* **M** *Mineral rich*

Put all the ingredients into a blender and blend until smooth.

MOCHA MACA

Makes: 1
Preparation: 5 minutes

YOU NEED

1 shot of espresso, cooled • 300 ml almond milk • 3 Medjool dates, pitted
1 banana, peeled • 1 tablespoon maca powder • a few drops of vanilla extract
pinch of ground cinnamon • 1 teaspoon cacao nibs • pinch of sea salt

Maca is a great source of nutrients, including over 20 amino acids of which 8 are essential.

E *Energising* **M** *Metabolism boosting* **P** *Protein boosting*

Put all the ingredients into a blender and blend until smooth.

GREEN BANANA

Makes: 1
Preparation: 5 minutes

YOU NEED

300 ml almond milk • 3 Medjool dates, pitted • 1 banana, peeled

1 teaspoon spirulina • ½ teaspoon vanilla extract

Spirulina is made up of 60 per cent protein and is rich in iron.

 *Vitamin rich* **E** *Energising* **M** *Mineral rich*

Put all the ingredients into a blender and blend until smooth.

COFFEE ALMOND

Makes: 1
Preparation: 5 minutes

YOU NEED

300 ml almond milk • 1 shot of espresso, cooled

3 Medjool dates, pitted • ½ teaspoon vanilla extract

Coffee is loaded with antioxidants. Coffee drinkers are said to be at a lower risk of several serious diseases.

P *Protein boosting* E *Energising* M *Metabolism boosting*

Put all the ingredients into a blender and blend until smooth.

WARM MANGO

Makes: 1
Preparation: 5 minutes

YOU NEED

300 ml cashew milk • 1 Medjool date, pitted • ½ mango, peeled and chopped
pinch of ground ginger • pinch of ground cinnamon

Mango helps lower cholesterol and improves digestion.

 V *Vitamin rich* P *Protein boosting* C *Calming*

Put all the ingredients into a blender and blend until smooth.

BEETROOT CACAO*

Makes: 1
Preparation: 5 minutes

YOU NEED
250 ml almond milk • 1 beetroot, juiced • 1 teaspoon cacao powder
1 Medjool date, pitted • 1 teaspoon honey

36

Beetroot is a great source of iron and folate.

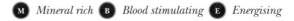 Mineral rich B Blood stimulating E Energising

Put all the ingredients into a blender and blend until smooth.

EARTHY ALMOND*

Makes: 1
Preparation: 10 minutes

YOU NEED
1 beetroot, peeled • ¼ pineapple, peeled • ¼ cucumber
1 pickled slice of jalapeño chilli • 1 teaspoon maca powder
splash of almond milk

Pineapple is great at building strong bones and is also good for keeping your eyes healthy.

A *Anti-inflammatory* **E** *Energising* **R** *Rehydrating*

Juice the beetroot, pineapple and cucumber, then pour the juice into a blender. Add the chilli and maca powder with the almond milk and blend for 30 seconds.

BLUEBERRY FLAX

Makes: 1
Preparation: 5 minutes

YOU NEED
300 ml almond milk • handful of blueberries • 1 teaspoon blueberry powder
1 teaspoon ground flaxseed • 1 teaspoon açaí berry powder

Blueberries are rich in potassium, folate and vitamins C and B6, which all support a healthy heart.

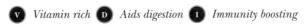 *Vitamin rich* **D** *Aids digestion* **I** *Immunity boosting*

Put all the ingredients into a blender and blend until smooth.

BERRY BAOBAB

Makes: 1
Preparation: 5 minutes

YOU NEED
300 ml almond milk • 150 g frozen mixed berries
1 tablespoon baobab powder • 1 teaspoon chia seeds

Baobab is rich in antioxidants and is a great source of calcium, potassium, thiamin and vitamin B6.

V *Vitamin rich* **P** *Protein boosting* **E** *Energising*

Put all the ingredients into a blender and blend until smooth.

SIMPLE GREEN*

Makes: 1
Preparation: 5 minutes

YOU NEED

handful of spinach • 2 celery sticks • 1 apple, cored

250 ml almond milk • 1 tablespoon honey

Spinach is rich in antioxidants and is a great source of vitamins A, B2, C and K.

 *Protein boosting* **M** *Mineral rich* **C** *Cleansing*

Juice the spinach, celery and apple. Add the almond milk and honey to the juice and stir thoroughly.

SUPER KALE*

Makes: 1
Preparation: 5 minutes

YOU NEED
handful of spinach • handful of kale • ½ cucumber
1 apple, cored • 250 ml brown rice milk • 1 tablespoon honey

Kale has a rich fibre content, which helps digestion.

V *Vitamin rich* **M** *Mineral rich* **I** *Immunity boosting*

Juice the spinach, kale, cucumber and apple. Add the juice to the rice milk with the honey and stir.

ICED MILKS

These summery super milks are packed full of protein and are finished with fruit and vegetables to add even more nutrients and give them a thicker texture. Please note that adding a handful of ice to each recipe in this chapter is beneficial.

Date • Strawberry Flax • Citrus Zing
Spinach Apple • Cacao Cinnamon
Mango Pineapple • Mocha Oatmeal
Almond Cacao • Cashew Cream • Banana
Vanilla Maca • Pink Berry • Cranberry Kefir
Maple Coffee • Cardamom & Rose

DATE

Makes: 1
Preparation: 5 minutes

YOU NEED

250 ml almond milk • 1 banana, peeled • 3 Medjool dates, pitted
1 teaspoon date syrup (optional) • pinch of ground nutmeg

Dates are great at relieving constipation and supporting regular bowel movements.

E *Energising* **P** *Protein boosting* **M** *Mineral rich*

Put all the ingredients into a blender with a handful of ice and blend until smooth.

STRAWBERRY FLAX

Makes: 1
Preparation: 5 minutes

YOU NEED

300 ml cashew milk • 6 strawberries, hulled • 1 tablespoon ground flaxseed

Strawberries are not only high in vitamin C but also contain folate, potassium, manganese, dietary fibre and magnesium.

V *Vitamin rich* **P** *Protein boosting* **D** *Aids digestion*

Put all the ingredients into a blender with a handful of ice and blend until smooth.

CITRUS ZING

Makes: 1
Preparation: 5 minutes

YOU NEED
250 ml rice milk • 1 lemon, peeled • 1 cm piece of fresh ginger, peeled
1 tablespoon honey

Lemons contain a good amount of potassium, which is good for a healthy heart.

(A) *Alkalising* (M) *Metabolism boosting* (D) *Aids digestion*

Put all the ingredients into a blender with a handful of ice and blend until smooth.

SPINACH APPLE

Makes: 1
Preparation: 5 minutes

YOU NEED
250 ml oat milk • handful of spinach • 1 apple, peeled and cored
juice of ½ lime • 1 tablespoon honey • 2 mint sprigs

This power milk is low in fat and full of zinc, fibre and vitamins A, C, E, K and B6.

D *Aids digestion*   **V** *Vitamin rich*   **P** *Protein boosting*

Put all the ingredients into a blender with a handful of ice and blend until smooth.

CACAO CINNAMON

Makes: 1
Preparation: 5 minutes

YOU NEED

250 ml hazelnut milk • 2 Medjool dates, pitted • 1 tablespoon hazelnuts, skinned

1 teaspoon cacao powder • ½ teaspoon ground cinnamon

Cacao is full of antioxidants as well as being the biggest plant-based source of iron.

B *Blood stimulating* **P** *Protein boosting* **D** *Aids digestion*

Put all the ingredients into a blender with a handful of ice and blend until smooth.

MANGO PINEAPPLE

Makes: 1
Preparation: 5 minutes

YOU NEED

250 ml cashew milk • ½ mango, peeled and chopped

80 g pineapple, peeled and cut into chunks (fresh or frozen)

1 cm piece of fresh ginger, peeled

This power milk is packed full of vitamins to give your body an immunity boost.

Put all the ingredients into a blender with a handful of ice and blend until smooth.

MOCHA OATMEAL

Makes: 1
Preparation: 5 minutes

YOU NEED

250 ml oat milk • 1 espresso shot, cooled or 1 teaspoon instant coffee

2 tablespoons rolled oats • 1 tablespoon honey • 1 teaspoon cacao powder

Oats are a great source of nutrients and are beneficial if you suffer from coeliac disease as they are gluten free. They boost vitamin B1, plus magnesium and zinc.

P *Protein boosting*　**C** *Cholesterol lowering*　**D** *Aids digestion*

Put all the ingredients into a blender with a handful of ice and blend until smooth.

ALMOND CACAO

Makes: 1
Preparation: 5 minutes

YOU NEED

250 ml almond milk • 2 Medjool dates, pitted • 1 teaspoon cacao powder

Cacao is a natural mood enhancer, so try this power milk to boost your mood.

Put all the ingredients into a blender with a handful of ice and blend until smooth.

CASHEW CREAM

Makes: 1
Preparation: 5 minutes

YOU NEED
250 ml cashew milk • 2 Medjool dates, pitted
1 tablespoon cashew butter • 1 tablespoon cashews

Cashews can help the body fight against heart disease and prevent gallstones.

E *Energising* **S** *Stress busting* **M** *Mineral rich*

Put all the ingredients into a blender with a handful of ice and blend until smooth.

BANANA

Makes: 1
Preparation: 5 minutes

YOU NEED

250 ml oat milk • 1 banana, peeled • 1 teaspoon bee pollen • 1 teaspoon honey

Bananas are an excellent source of potassium, vitamins B6 and C, fibre and carbohydrate.

M *Mineral rich* **P** *Protein boosting* **B** *Bone strengthening*

Put all the ingredients into a blender with a handful of ice and blend until smooth.

VANILLA MACA

Makes: 1
Preparation: 20 minutes

YOU NEED

1 teaspoon chia seeds • 250 ml almond milk • 1 teaspoon vanilla extract

1 Medjool date, pitted • 1 teaspoon maca powder

Vanilla contains numerous antioxidants, as well as anti-inflammatory properties.

B *Brain boosting* **M** *Mineral rich* **B** *Bone strengthening*

Leave the chia seeds to soak in the almond milk for 15 minutes. Add the vanilla extract, date and maca powder to the chia seeds, then add everything to a blender. Blitz with a handful of ice and serve.

PINK BERRY

Makes: 1
Preparation: 5 minutes

YOU NEED
250 ml almond milk • 9 strawberries, hulled • 1 tablespoon blueberries
½ teaspoon vanilla extract

Berries are a great source of fibre, which is an important nutrient for a healthy digestive system.

V *Vitamin rich* **B** *Bone strengthening* **E** *Energising*

Put all the ingredients into a blender with a handful of ice and blend until smooth.

CRANBERRY KEFIR

Makes: 1
Preparation: 5 minutes

YOU NEED

250 ml milk kefir • 2 Medjool dates, pitted

2 tablespoons dried cranberries • ½ teaspoon cacao powder

Kefir contains high levels of vitamin B12, calcium, magnesium and folate.

P *Probiotic* **S** *Skin enhancing* **P** *Purifying*

Put all the ingredients into a blender with a handful of ice and blend until smooth.

MAPLE COFFEE

Makes: 1
Preparation: 5 minutes

YOU NEED

250 ml almond milk • 1 shot of espresso or 1 teaspoon instant coffee

1 tablespoon maple syrup

Coffee is filled with antioxidants, which in turn gives your mood a boost.

Ⓜ *Metabolism boosting* Ⓜ *Mineral rich* Ⓑ *Brain boosting*

Put all the ingredients into a blender with a handful of ice and blend until smooth.

CARDAMOM & ROSE

Makes: 1
Preparation: 15 minutes

YOU NEED

250 ml coconut milk • 1 teaspoon dried rose petals • 1 teaspoon honey

a pinch of ground cardamom

Cardamom can help prevent bloating, gas and heartburn. It also helps the body to eliminate waste through the kidneys.

B *Bone strengthening* **S** *Skin enhancing* **L** *Liver cleansing*

Put all the ingredients into a saucepan and slowly bring to just under a simmer. Turn off the heat and leave to stand for 2 minutes before pouring through a sieve into a blender. Add a handful of ice and blend until smooth.

HEALING MILKS

*These functional superfood milks add
some warmth to your wellness routine.
They are not only comforting, but
loaded with restorative ingredients too.*

The Psychedelic • Magic Mushroom
Spiced Cacao • Chamomile Coconut
Lavender Almond • Maca Maple
Coconut Karma • Turmeric Treat
Sea of Coconut • Beet the Milk
Rose Chocolate • Ginger Ninja
Cinnamon Secret • Hazelnut Halo
Brazilian Beauty • Chaga Mix

THE PSYCHEDELIC

Makes: 1
Preparation: 5 minutes + Heating: 5 minutes

YOU NEED

250 ml coconut milk • juice of ½ lemon • ½ teaspoon ground ginger
½ teaspoon spirulina • pinch of ground turmeric
pinch of pomegranate powder

This milk soothes the body and helps stimulate the blood while containing good levels of calcium and iron.

(A) *Anti-inflammatory* (I) *Immunity boosting* (C) *Calming*

Bring the coconut milk to a simmer in a saucepan with the lemon juice, ground ginger and spirulina. Pour into a cup and sprinkle with the turmeric and pomegranate powder.

MAGIC MUSHROOM

Makes: 1
Preparation: 5 minutes + Heating: 5 minutes

YOU NEED

250 ml coconut milk • 1 teaspoon maca powder

1 teaspoon honey • ¼ teaspoon reishi powder, plus a pinch for sprinkling

¼ teaspoon cordycep powder, plus a pinch for sprinkling

¼ teaspoon chaga powder, plus a pinch for sprinkling

Mushroom powders not only help your immune system but are also good for balancing hormone levels.

 *Immunity boosting*  *Calming* *Mood boosting*

Bring all the ingredients to a simmer in a saucepan. Stir and pour into a cup. Sprinkle with the extra pinches of the mushroom powders.

SPICED CACAO

Makes: 1
Preparation: 5 minutes + Heating: 5 minutes

YOU NEED

300 ml almond milk • 1 teaspoon cacao powder • 1 teaspoon maple syrup
½ teaspoon ground cinnamon • ½ teaspoon hemp powder
½ teaspoon vanilla extract • pinch of ground cardamom
pinch of ground nutmeg

This hot milk is great to enjoy for full relaxation. Not only is it good for you but it will also help your brain slow down after a hard day.

S *Stress busting* **C** *Cholesterol lowering* **V** *Vitamin rich*

Bring all the ingredients to a simmer in a saucepan, stirring occasionally. Once heated, pour into a heatproof cup and serve.

CHAMOMILE COCONUT

Makes: 1
Preparation: 5 minutes + Heating: 5 minutes

YOU NEED

300 ml coconut milk • 1 teaspoon honey • 1 teaspoon collagen protein powder
1 teaspoon dried chamomile flowers • 1 teaspoon camu camu powder
½ teaspoon sea buckthorn powder • ¼ teaspoon ground ginger
¼ teaspoon ground turmeric

This beauty milk is full of protein and helps improve blood pressure. Bursting with vitamin C from the camu camu powder; make this part of your skincare routine.

S *Skin enhancing* **I** *Immunity boosting* **L** *Liver cleansing*

Bring all the ingredients to a simmer in a saucepan, stirring occasionally. Once heated, strain into a cup and serve.

LAVENDER ALMOND

Makes: 1
Preparation: 5 minutes + Heating: 5 minutes

YOU NEED

250 ml almond milk • 1 teaspoon dried lavender • ½ teaspoon maqui berry powder
½ teaspoon vanilla extract • ½ teaspoon lucuma powder

This super-nutritious milk is full of ingredients to fight free radicals and boost your mood.

A *High in antioxidants* **D** *Aids digestion* **P** *Protein boosting*

Bring all the ingredients to a simmer in a saucepan, stirring occasionally. Once heated, strain into a heatproof cup and serve.

MACA MAPLE

Makes: 1
Preparation: 5 minutes + Heating: 5 minutes

YOU NEED
250 ml cashew milk • 1 tablespoon maca powder
1 tablespoon cashew butter • 1 teaspoon blueberry powder

This soothing milk is full of vitamins that help support a healthy heart.

P *Protein boosting* **B** *Bone strengthening* **I** *Immunity boosting*

Bring all the ingredients to a simmer in a saucepan, stirring occasionally.
Once heated, pour into a heatproof cup and serve.

COCONUT KARMA

Makes: 1
Preparation: 5 minutes + Heating: 5 minutes

YOU NEED

250 ml coconut milk • 1 teaspoon coconut butter • 1 teaspoon cacao powder
1 teaspoon maple syrup • ½ teaspoon vanilla extract • ½ teaspoon camu camu powder

Camu camu powder is high in antioxidants and helps balance your mood.

S *Soothing* **L** *Liver cleansing* **A** *Anti-inflammatory*

Bring all the ingredients to a simmer in a saucepan and stir.
Once heated, pour into a heatproof cup and serve.

TURMERIC TREAT

Makes: 1
Preparation: 5 minutes + Heating: 5 minutes

YOU NEED
150 ml almond milk • 1 teaspoon honey • ½ teaspoon ground turmeric
pinch of ground cinnamon

This warming anti-inflammatory milk is a perfect calming drink before sleep.

I *Immunity boosting* **P** *Protein boosting* **B** *Blood pressure lowering*

Bring all the ingredients, together with 150 ml water, to a slow simmer
in a saucepan. Once heated, pour into a heatproof cup and serve.

SEA OF COCONUT

Makes: 1
Preparation: 5 minutes + Heating: 7 minutes

YOU NEED

150 ml coconut milk • 1 teaspoon matcha (green tea) powder

1 teaspoon coconut sugar • pinch of spirulina

Matcha (green tea) powder gives a great boost to your metabolism, helping you to burn calories.

S *Skin enhancing* **M** *Mood enhancing* **D** *Aids digestion*

Bring all the ingredients, together with 150 ml water, to a simmer in a saucepan. Simmer for 2 minutes, then stir, pour into a heatproof cup and serve.

BEET THE MILK

Makes: 1
Preparation: 5 minutes + Heating: 7 minutes

YOU NEED

150 ml almond milk • 1 teaspoon beetroot powder • 1 teaspoon maple syrup
½ teaspoon vanilla extract

This soothing milk helps lower cholesterol, giving a boost to your heart health.

V *Vitamin rich* P *Protein boosting* D *Aids digestion*

Bring all the ingredients, together with 150 ml water, to a simmer in a saucepan.
Simmer for 2 minutes, then stir, pour into a heatproof cup and serve.

ROSE CHOCOLATE

Makes: 1
Preparation: 5 minutes + Heating: 7 minutes

YOU NEED
150 ml cashew milk • 1 teaspoon dried rose petals • 1 teaspoon cacao powder
1 teaspoon maple syrup • few drops of rose water (optional)

Rose is a great anti-viral, so try this when you have a sore throat or a cold.

 *Energising* C *Calming* B *Blood stimulating*

Bring all the ingredients, together with 150 ml water, to a simmer in a saucepan.
Simmer for 2 minutes, then stir, strain into a heatproof cup and serve.

GINGER NINJA

Makes: 1
Preparation: 5 minutes + Heating: 7 minutes

YOU NEED

150 ml coconut milk • ½ teaspoon ground ginger • pinch of ground nutmeg
pinch of ground cloves • pinch of cayenne pepper

This soothing milk will help relieve digestive problems such as nausea, loss of appetite, motion sickness and pain.

B *Blood stimulating* **I** *Immunity boosting* **R** *Revitalising*

Bring all the ingredients, together with 150 ml water, to a simmer in a saucepan. Simmer for 2 minutes, then pour into a heatproof cup and serve.

CINNAMON SECRET

Makes: 1
Preparation: 5 minutes + Heating: 7 minutes

YOU NEED
250 ml cashew milk • 1 teaspoon almond butter
1 teaspoon maple syrup • 1 cinnamon stick or ½ teaspoon ground cinnamon

Cinnamon contains anti-inflammatory properties as well as helping the body fight infections and viruses.

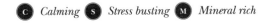 *Calming* Ⓢ *Stress busting* Ⓜ *Mineral rich*

Bring all the ingredients to a simmer in a saucepan. Simmer for 2 minutes, then pour into a cup. Remove the cinnamon stick and serve.

HAZELNUT HALO

Makes: 1
Preparation: 5 minutes + Heating: 7 minutes

YOU NEED

250 ml hazelnut milk • 1 tablespoon hazelnut butter • ½ teaspoon cacao powder

Hazelnuts are great for maintaining healthy skin, hair and nails because of their high vitamin E content. They also contain B vitamins, which boost metabolism.

S *Skin enhancing* **M** *Mineral rich* **P** *Protein boosting*

Bring all the ingredients to a simmer in a saucepan. Simmer for 2 minutes, then pour into a heatproof cup and serve.

BRAZILIAN BEAUTY

Makes: 1
Preparation: 5 minutes + Heating: 7 minutes

YOU NEED

250 ml Brazil nut milk • 1 teaspoon collagen protein powder
1 teaspoon date syrup • pinch of cacao powder

Brazil nuts are the best source of selenium, which is a trace mineral essential for the immune system. It also plays a role in male and female fertility.

B *Bone strengthening* **P** *Protein boosting* **D** *Aids digestion*

Bring all the ingredients to a simmer in a saucepan. Simmer for 2 minutes, then pour into a heatproof cup and serve.

CHAGA MIX

Makes: 1
Preparation: 5 minutes + Heating: 7 minutes

YOU NEED
250 ml almond milk • 1 teaspoon chaga powder • 1 teaspoon honey
½ teaspoon cashew butter

Chaga mushroom powder contains polysaccharides, which help provide cells with energy and improve heart health, along with promoting healthy blood sugar levels.

(A) *High in antioxidants* **(E)** *Energising* **(C)** *Cholesterol lowering*

Bring all the ingredients to a simmer in a saucepan. Simmer for 2 minutes, then pour into a heatproof cup and serve.

TEA MILKS

*Made from a combination of tea
blends, Ayurvedic herbs and spices
whipped up to relieve stress and
restore balance.*

Early Rose • Anise Vanilla • Mulberry
Green Ashwa • Matcha Plus • Honey Saffron
Fennel Fruit • Rosemary Cacao • All Spiced Up
Coriander Orange • Barley Root
Juniper Refresh • Clover Leaf • Mint Ease
Liquorice • Chamomile • Green Coco
Maple Chai • Vanilla Turmeric
Early Grey Mocha • Minty Hibiscus

EARLY ROSE

Makes: 1
Preparation: 5 minutes + Steeping: 3 minutes

YOU NEED

1 Earl Grey teabag • few drops of rose water • splash of coconut milk

½ teaspoon dried rose petals

This tea milk helps relieve tension and fatigue.

C *Calming* **H** *Hydrating* **S** *Stress busting*

Pour 300 ml boiling water over the Earl Grey teabag and rose water in a heatproof jug and leave to steep for 3 minutes. Remove the bag, add the coconut milk and garnish with a few dried rose petals to serve.

ANISE VANILLA

Makes: 1
Preparation: 5 minutes + Steeping: 3 minutes

YOU NEED

1 teaspoon anise • ½ teaspoon vanilla extract • splash of coconut milk

Anise is an excellent remedy for asthma and bronchitis as well as digestive disorders.

H *Hydrating* **B** *Blood enhancing* **C** *Cleansing*

Pour 300 ml boiling water over the anise and vanilla extract in a heatproof jug and leave to steep for 3 minutes. Strain into a heatproof cup and add the coconut milk to serve.

MULBERRY

Makes: 1
Preparation: 5 minutes + Steeping: 5 minutes

YOU NEED

1 mulberry teabag or 1 teaspoon mulberry leaf tea • splash of oat milk
pinch of goji berry powder

Mulberries are full of nutrients including vitamins C and K, and are a great support for the immune system.

A *High in antioxidants* **M** *Mineral rich* **H** *Hydrating*

Pour 300 ml boiling water over the mulberry teabag or tea in a heatproof jug and leave to steep for 5 minutes. Strain into a cup and add the oat milk and goji berry powder, then serve.

GREEN ASHWA

Makes: 1
Preparation: 5 minutes + Steeping: 5 minutes

YOU NEED

1 green tea teabag • 1 teaspoon ashwagandha powder

pinch of ground cinnamon • pinch of cayenne pepper

½ teaspoon ho shou wu or fo-ti powder (optional) • 1 teaspoon honey

splash of coconut milk

This metabolism-boosting tea milk cleanses the liver and kidneys.

 *Anti-inflammatory* **B** *Blood stimulating* **S** *Stress busting*

Put all the ingredients, except the milk, in a saucepan and add 300 ml boiling water.
Leave to steep for 5 minutes. Remove the teabag, pour into a cup and add the
coconut milk to serve.

MATCHA PLUS

Makes: 1
Preparation: 5 minutes + Steeping: 5 minutes

YOU NEED
1 teaspoon matcha (green tea) powder • ½ teaspoon vanilla extract
½ teaspoon lucuma powder • a splash of coconut milk

Matcha (green tea) powder is great for increasing your energy levels and boosting your endurance.

Ⓜ *Metabolism boosting* Ⓑ *Brain boosting* Ⓘ *Immunity boosting*

Pour 300 ml boiling water over the matcha, vanilla extract and lucuma powder in a heatproof jug and leave to steep for 5 minutes. Add the coconut milk, stir and serve.

HONEY SAFFRON

Makes: 1
Preparation: 5 minutes + Steeping: 5 minutes

YOU NEED
½ teaspoon saffron powder or pinch of saffron strands • 1 teaspoon honey
pinch of freshly ground black pepper • splash of coconut milk

Saffron is loaded with minerals from potassium, calcium and manganese to iron and selenium.

M *Mood enhancing* **S** *Stress busting* **C** *Calming*

Pour 300 ml boiling water over the saffron, honey and black pepper in a heatproof jug and leave to steep for 5 minutes. Add the coconut milk and serve.

FENNEL FRUIT

Makes: 1
Preparation: 5 minutes + Steeping: 5 minutes

YOU NEED

1 fennel teabag or 1 teaspoon fennel seeds • ½ teaspoon pomegranate powder

splash of coconut milk

Fennel is a great reliever for irritable bowel syndrome as it calms the digestive system. It also helps to relieve hiccups.

V *Vitamin rich* **I** *Immunity boosting* **H** *Hydrating*

Pour 300 ml boiling water over the fennel and pomegranate powder in a heatproof jug and leave to steep for 5 minutes. Remove the teabag or strain into a cup. Add the coconut milk and serve.

ROSEMARY CACAO

Makes: 1
Preparation: 5 minutes + Steeping: 5 minutes

YOU NEED

1 rosemary sprig or 1 teaspoon dried rosemary leaves • ½ teaspoon cacao powder
1 teaspoon honey • splash of rice milk

Rosemary has two powerful antioxidant compounds present, which are linked to helping reduce inflammation in the body.

B *Blood boosting* **M** *Metabolism stimulating* **E** *Energising*

Pour 300 ml boiling water over the rosemary, cacao and honey in a heatproof jug and leave to steep for 5 minutes. Strain into a cup, add the rice milk and serve.

ALL SPICED UP

Makes: 1
Preparation: 5 minutes + Steeping: 5 minutes

YOU NEED
1 teaspoon dried allspice berries • a pinch of ground cinnamon
1 teaspoon honey • ½ teaspoon grated orange peel • a splash of oat milk

Allspice berries are good for calming your digestion and improving circulation.

B *Brain boosting* **M** *Mineral rich* **D** *Aids digestion*

Pour 300 ml boiling water over the berries, cinnamon, honey and orange peel in a
heatproof jug. Leave for 5 minutes. Strain into a cup, add the oat milk and serve.

CORIANDER ORANGE

Makes: 1
Preparation: 5 minutes + Steeping: 5 minutes

YOU NEED

1 teaspoon coriander seeds • 1 shaving of orange peel • 1 teaspoon lemon juice
1 tablespoon orange juice • 1 teaspoon honey • splash of coconut milk

Coriander can help with urinary tract infections, decreasing blood pressure and lowering blood sugar.

 *Mineral rich* **A** *Alkalising* **D** *Aids digestion*

Pour 300 ml boiling water over all the ingredients, except the milk, in a heatproof jug and leave for 5 minutes. Strain into a cup, add the coconut milk and serve.

BARLEY ROOT

Makes: 1
Preparation: 5 minutes + Heating: 10 minutes + Steeping: 5 minutes

YOU NEED

1 tablespoon raw or toasted barley • pinch of ground ginger

1 teaspoon honey (optional) • splash of rice milk

Barley tea has antibacterial properties and improves blood circulation.

 Blood stimulating  Body balancing  Purifying

If using raw barley, fry in a dry frying pan for 5 minutes, or until toasted. Add the toasted barley to a saucepan with the ginger, honey and 300 ml boiling water and bring to a simmer. Simmer for 5 minutes. Remove from the heat and leave to steep for 5 minutes. Strain into a cup and top with the rice milk.

JUNIPER REFRESH

Makes: 1
Preparation: 5 minutes + Steeping: 5 minutes

YOU NEED

1 tablespoon juniper berries • ½ teaspoon maqui berry powder
½ teaspoon açaí berry powder • 1 teaspoon honey (optional)
splash of coconut milk

Juniper berries have a calming and diuretic-type effect on the body.

I *Immunity boosting* **V** *Vitamin rich* **S** *Skin enhancing*

Pour 300 ml boiling water over all the ingredients, except the milk, in a heatproof jug. Leave for 5 minutes. Strain into a cup, add the coconut milk and serve.

CLOVER LEAF

Makes: 1
Preparation: 5 minutes + Steeping: 5 minutes

YOU NEED
1 tablespoon loose red clover tea • 1 strip of orange peel • 1 teaspoon honey
splash of coconut milk

Red clover is a rich source of isoflavones, which are chemicals known as phytoestrogens and are used to help hot flushes and pre-menstrual syndrome.

B *Brain boosting* **B** *Blood boosting* **S** *Stress busting*

Pour 300 ml boiling water over all the ingredients, except the milk, in a heatproof jug. Leave for 5 minutes. Strain into a cup, add the coconut milk and serve.

MINT EASE

Makes: 1
Preparation: 5 minutes + Steeping: 5 minutes

YOU NEED

3 mint sprigs or a mint teabag • pinch of matcha (green tea) powder
splash of rice milk

Mint helps relax the body and mind, as well as helping to reduce inflammation and boost the immune system.

C *Calming* **D** *Aids digestion* **L** *Liver cleansing*

Pour 300 ml boiling water over the mint and matcha powder in a heatproof jug. Leave for 5 minutes. Strain into a cup, add the rice milk and serve.

LIQUORICE

Makes: 1
Preparation: 5 minutes + Steeping: 5 minutes

YOU NEED
1 tablespoon chopped liquorice root • 1 mint sprig • 1 teaspoon honey (optional)
splash of coconut milk

Liquorice helps with an upset stomach as well as easing the common cold.

Ⓒ *Calming* Ⓒ *Cholesterol lowering* Ⓓ *Aids digestion*

Pour 300 ml boiling water over all the ingredients, except the milk, in a heatproof jug and leave for 5 minutes. Strain into a cup, add the coconut milk and serve.

CHAMOMILE

Makes: 1
Preparation: 5 minutes + Steeping: 5 minutes

YOU NEED

1 teaspoon dried chamomile flowers • 1 tablespoon apple juice

splash of coconut milk

Chamomile helps ease anxiety and depression and is a natural allergy fighter.

D *Aids digestion* **A** *Anti-inflammatory* **S** *Skin enhancing*

Pour 300 ml boiling water over the chamomile and apple in a heatproof jug and
leave to steep for 5 minutes. Strain into a cup, add the coconut milk and serve.

GREEN COCO

Makes: 1
Preparation: 5 minutes + Heating: 3 minutes

YOU NEED

150 ml coconut milk • 1 tablespoon coconut butter

1 teaspoon matcha (green tea) powder • 1 teaspoon superfood greens powder

1 teaspoon honey • drop of vanilla extract

Matcha (green) tea is rich in fibre, chlorophyll and vitamins and will leave you feeling calm but alert.

E *Energising* **S** *Stress busting* **B** *Bone strengthening*

Bring the coconut milk to a simmer in a saucepan. Add the remaining ingredients to the hot milk and stir. Pour into a cup and top with boiling water to serve.

MAPLE CHAI

Makes: 1
Preparation: 5 minutes + Heating: 3 minutes + Steeping: 3 minutes

YOU NEED

300 ml coconut milk • 1 chai teabag • 1 tablespoon maple syrup

a drop of vanilla extract • pinch of ground cinnamon • pinch of ground nutmeg

The black tea in chai is loaded with antioxidants that can help prevent cardiovascular disease.

M *Mineral rich* **P** *Protein boosting* **I** *Immunity boosting*

Heat the coconut milk in a saucepan until just before it simmers. Add the chai teabag, stir and leave to steep for 3 minutes. Remove the teabag and add the remaining ingredients. Stir, then pour into a cup and serve.

VANILLA TURMERIC

Makes: 1
Preparation: 5 minutes + Heating: 5 minutes

YOU NEED

300 ml coconut milk • 1 teaspoon honey • ½ teaspoon vanilla extract
½ teaspoon coconut oil • ¼ teaspoon ground turmeric • ¼ teaspoon ground ginger
pinch of ground cinnamon • pinch of freshly ground black pepper

Turmeric is said to be good for stabilising your mood. It also helps to balance your blood sugar levels.

M *Mineral rich* **I** *Immunity boosting* **A** *Anti-inflammatory*

Pour the coconut milk into a saucepan, add the remaining ingredients and heat until just before it simmers. Heat for 5 minutes, whisking occasionally. Remove from the heat, pour into a cup and serve.

EARLY GREY MOCHA

Makes: 1
Preparation: 5 minutes + Heating: 3 minutes

YOU NEED

250 ml coconut milk • 1 Earl Grey teabag
1 espresso shot or ½ teaspoon instant coffee • 1 teaspoon dried rose petals
1 teaspoon honey (optional) • drop of rose petal essence

Earl Grey tea has a soothing and anti-inflammatory effect on the body.

M *Metabolism boosting* **D** *Aids digestion* **P** *Protein boosting*

Heat the coconut milk in a saucepan to just before it simmers, then add the Earl Grey teabag. Heat for 3 minutes. Remove the teabag and add the remaining ingredients. Stir, pour into a cup and serve.

MINTY HIBISCUS

Makes: 1
Preparation: 15 minutes + Steeping: 3 minutes

YOU NEED
1 tablespoon hibiscus tea leaves • 2 mint sprigs • 1 teaspoon honey
splash of coconut milk

Hibiscus tea can help decrease your body temperature and aid in the treatment of high blood pressure.

M *Metabolism boosting* **I** *Immunity boosting* **D** *Aids digestion*

Pour 250 ml hot water over the hibiscus and mint in a heatproof jug and leave for 5 minutes. Strain into a cup and serve with the honey and coconut milk.

INDEX

Acknowledgements

A big thank you to Deidre Rooney for her fab photos in this book, and also a big thanks to Kathy Steer and Michelle Tilly for their tenacity and patience. This book wouldn't have happened if it wasn't for the help of my husband Jono. I love you always.

The author has researched each plant, superfood and complementary medicine powder used in this book but is not responsible for any adverse effects the plants or powders may have on an individual. One plant may be good for one person but have a negative effect on another. All the plants and powders are consumed entirely at your own risk. Never use anything as an alternative to seeking professional medical advice and always consume in moderation. Please speak to your doctor if you have any concerns with regards to taking any of the complementary medicine powders in this book.

First published in 2017 by © Hachette Livre (Marabout)

The English language edition published in 2018 by Hardie Grant Books, an imprint of Hardie Grant Publishing

Hardie Grant Books (London)
5th & 6th Floors
52–54 Southwark Street
London SE1 1UN

Hardie Grant Books (Melbourne)
Building 1, 658 Church Street
Richmond, Victoria 3121

hardiegrantbooks.com

Text © Fern Green
Photography © Deidre Rooney

British Library Cataloguing-in-Publication Data.
A catalogue record for this book is available from the British Library.

Power Milks by Fern Green

ISBN 978-1-78488-201-3

Publisher: Catie Ziller
Photography: Deidre Rooney
Designer: Michelle Tilly
Editor: Kathy Steer

For the English hardback edition:

Publishing Director: Kate Pollard
Junior Editor: Eila Purvis
Editor: Amy Christian
Colour Reproduction by p2d

Printed and bound in China by
Leo Paper Group